FARM ANIMALS

PIGS

Written by Sadie Hallworth

Genius Kid

This edition is published by arrangement with BookLife Publishing

sales@northstareditions.com | 888-417-0195

Library of Congress Control Number:
The Library of Congress Control Number is available on the Library of Congress website.

ISBN
979-8-89471-057-0 (library bound)
979-8-89471-077-8 (paperback)
979-8-89471-115-7 (epub)
979-8-89471-097-6 (hosted ebook)

Printed in the United States of America
Mankato, MN
012026

Written by:
Sadie Hallworth

Edited by:
Elise Carraway

Designed by:
Ker Ker Lee

Photo Credits – Images courtesy of Shutterstock.com, unless otherwise stated.

Cover – cynoclub, Eric Isselee, chrisbrignell, photomaster, Svetlana Foote, Stepnext. 2–3 – Dmitry Kalinovsky, photomaster. 4–5 – Eric Isselee. 6–7 – Eric Isselee. 8–9 – Sonsedska Yuliia, Eric Isselee, WildMedia. 10–11 – Jessica Sunderman, Eric Isselee, Nynke van Holten, cynoclub. 12–13 – Maksim Safaniuk, Mark William Richardson, Budimir Jevtic, Photoongraphy, wallerichmercie, andrefronza. 14–15 – janenero, GSDesign, Sergiy Kuzmin, New Africa, Nor Gal, bigjom jom. 16–17 – LittlePerfectStock, Olga_i. 18–19 – AIPhotoss, Aleksandar Malivuk. 20–21 – Eric Isselee, GoodFocused, Macab52, Cavan-Images. 22–23 – lera lysenko, Sorapop Udomsri, Sonsedska Yuliia, Oleksandr Lytvynenko, photomaster, Litvalifa.

CONTENTS

Words that look like <u>this</u> can be found in the glossary on page 24.

PIGS

Close your eyes and picture a pig. What do you see?

What color is its skin? Can you see a curly tail and a sniffing snout?

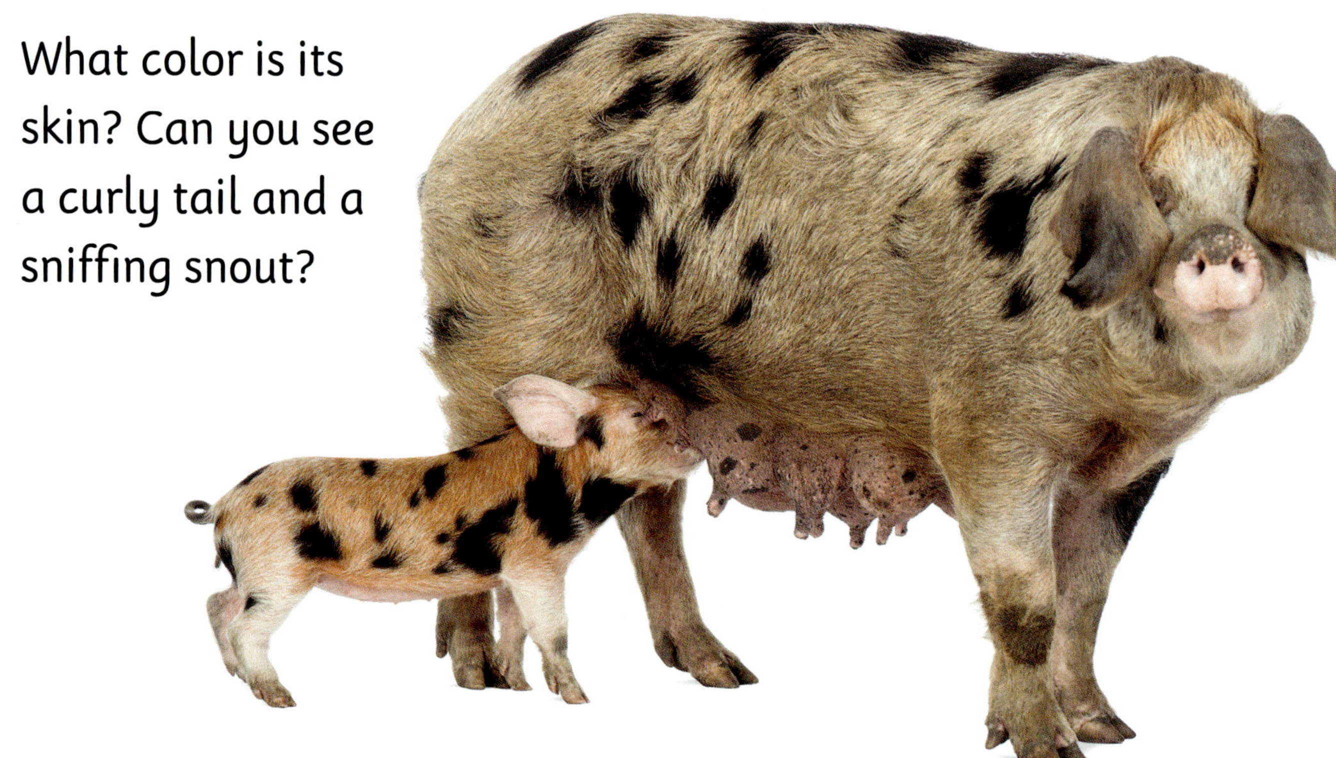

Pigs are mammals. They are warm-blooded, have a backbone, and make milk to feed their young.

Pig are omnivores. Omnivores are animals that eat plants and meat.

Many pigs are wild animals. However, most pigs are domesticated. They are kept by humans. Most domestic pigs live on farms.

BODY OF A PIG

Some pigs have thin, tightly curled tails.

Each foot has four toes covered by hooves. Hooves are made of keratin, which is the same thing human fingernails are made of. Pigs walk on the two largest hooves on the front of each foot.

DID YOU KNOW?
All hooved animals are called ungulates.

Pigs have very large bodies. Most wild pigs usually weigh around 75 to 250 pounds (34 to 113 kg). Large domestic pigs can weigh more than 700 pounds (320 kg).

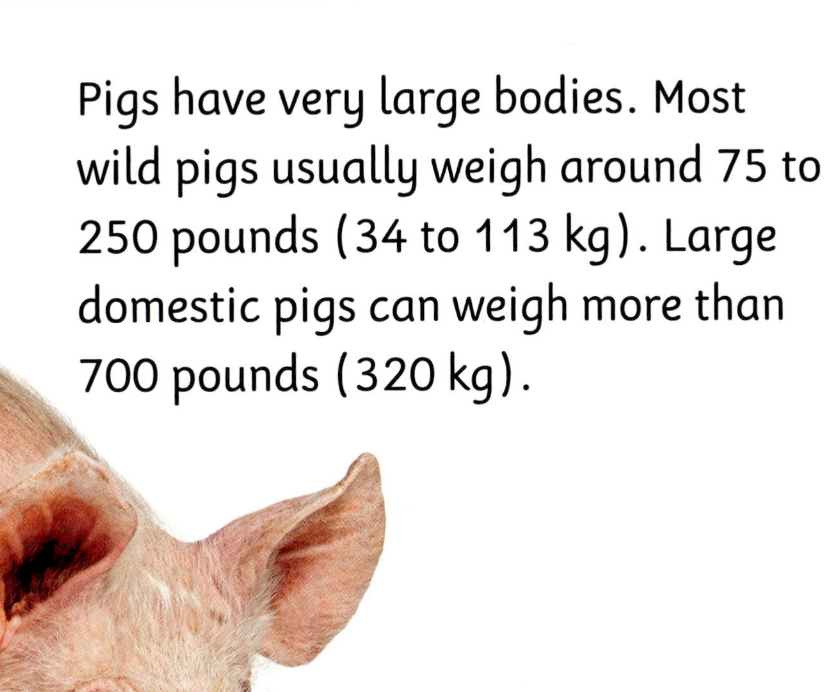

Like all mammals, pigs are covered with hair. Pig hair is often stiff and wiry.

Pigs have short legs.

FACE OF A PIG

Pigs have large ears.

Pigs' eyes are a bit like human eyes. They are about the same size and shape. Pigs' eyes are on the sides of their faces. They can see almost all around themselves.

Pigs are known for their flat noses, called snouts. They use their snouts to sniff and dig in the ground. Pigs have a very strong sense of smell.

Wild pigs have long teeth called tusks. Domestic pigs often have tusk-like teeth.

A wild pig's tusks

BREEDS OF PIGS

There are many types of pigs. Different types are called breeds. Breeds are created and controlled by humans. Humans develop each breed to have certain characteristics.

Hampshire pigs are mostly black with a white belt around their shoulders and front legs.

Yorkshire pigs are the most common type of pig in North America.

Mangalica pigs have curly hair that looks like sheep's wool.

Kunekune pigs come in many different colors.

Wild pigs usually have thicker hair than domestic pigs.

DID YOU KNOW?
Wild pigs are often known as wild boars.

LIFE ON THE FARM

On farms, most pigs live inside buildings called barns.

DID YOU KNOW?

Wild pigs live in many different habitats, including grasslands, wetlands, and forests.

Some farmed pigs live outside in fenced-off areas called pigpens or pigsties.

On the farm, pigs mostly eat food made of corn, wheat, soybeans, or barley. However, pigs will eat almost anything. If they got the chance, they would eat wild plants and even small animals.

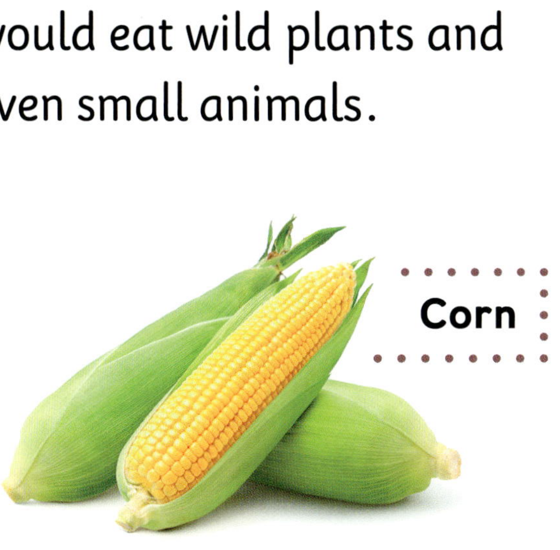

Corn

Soybeans

Wheat

DID YOU KNOW?

Pigs dig for food with their snouts. This is called rooting.

HOW PEOPLE USE PIGS

Most farmed pigs are made into food.

Meat that comes from pigs is called pork. Pork is often used to make sausages, bacon, and ham.

Some farm pigs are used to make lard. Lard is animal fat that is used for cooking and baking.

Pig skin is sometimes used to make a material called leather.

Thick boar hairs are called bristles. Boar bristles are sometimes used to make hairbrushes.

FROM PIGLET TO PIG

Pigs go through different stages throughout their lives.

Young pigs are called piglets. A group of them all born at the same time and to the same mother is called a litter. There are usually around 12 piglets in each litter.

Piglets drink milk from their mothers. On farms, piglets stop drinking milk at around three weeks old.

Pet pigs can live for up to 20 years. Farmed pigs live for around seven months.

LOOKING AFTER PIGS

Like all domestic animals, pigs need to be cared for. This may include visits from a vet.

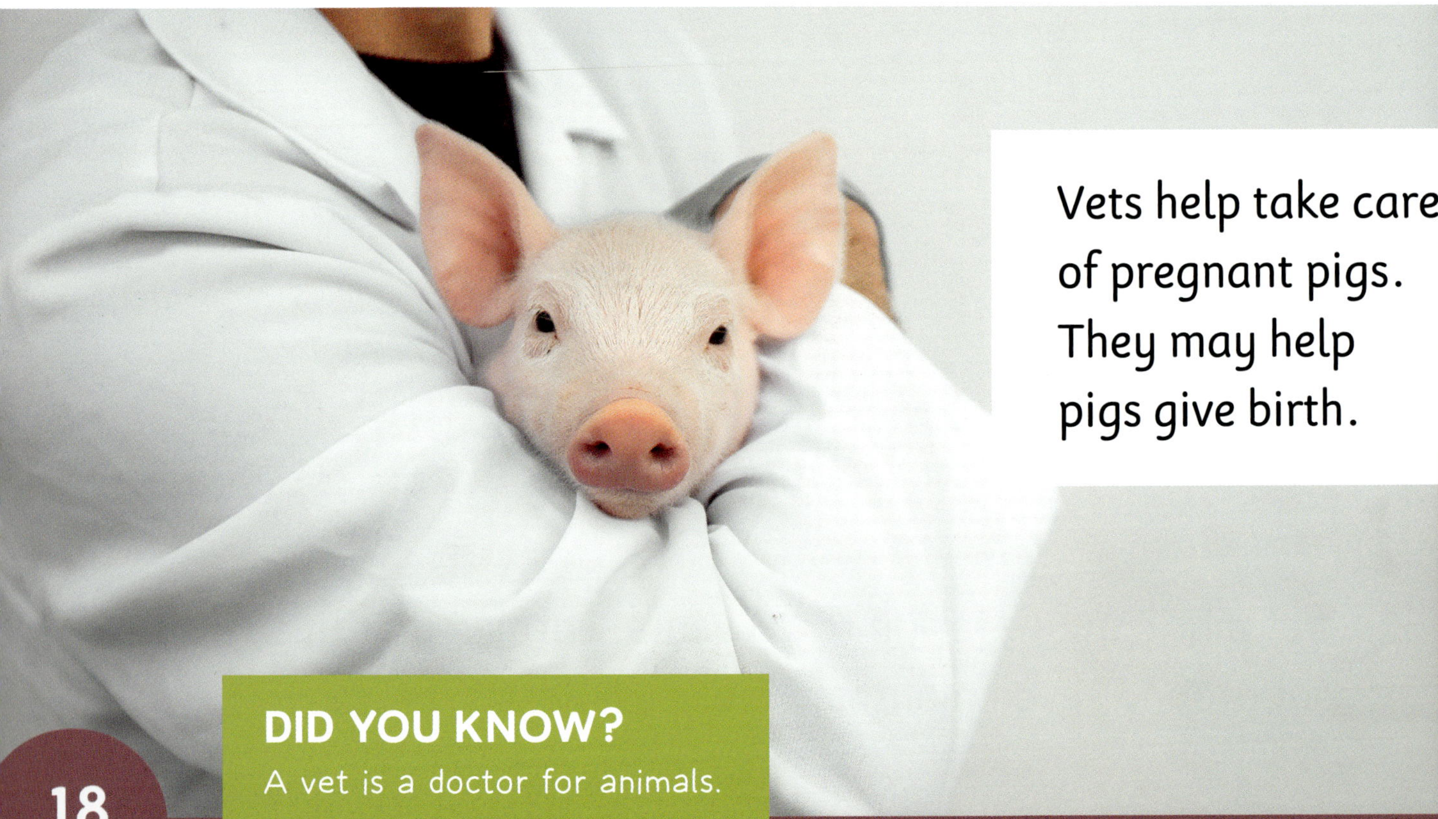

Vets help take care of pregnant pigs. They may help pigs give birth.

DID YOU KNOW?

A vet is a doctor for animals.

Vets help pigs stay healthy. They check for signs of illness. They may vaccinate the pigs.

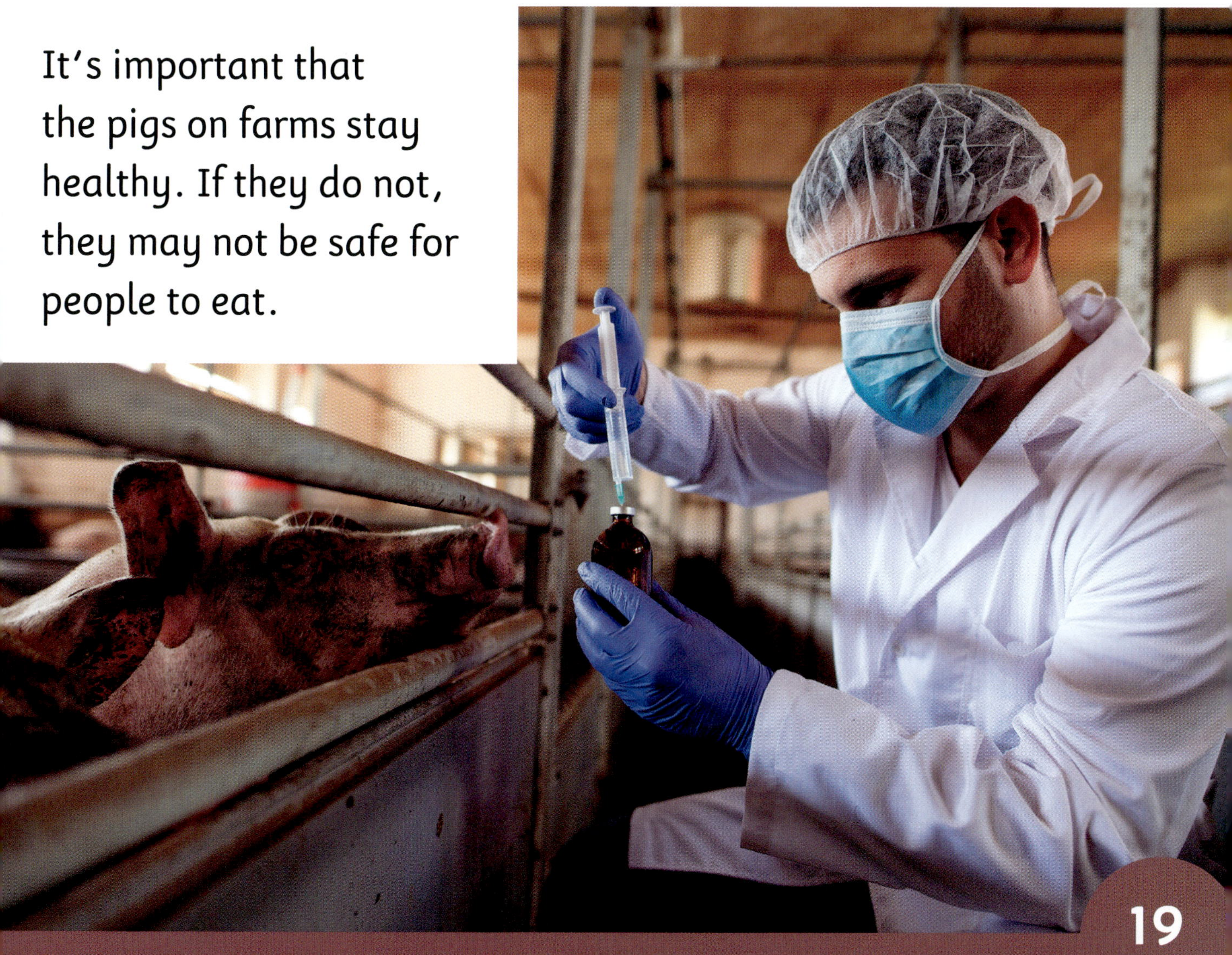

It's important that the pigs on farms stay healthy. If they do not, they may not be safe for people to eat.

BELIEVE IT OR NOT!

Pigs are some of the most intelligent domesticated animals. They are even smarter than dogs! Pigs can learn their names and how to play simple video games.

Most people think pigs only oink. However, they can communicate using around 20 different sounds.

Pigs are known for rolling around in mud, but they are not dirty animals. Pigs don't sweat very much, so they roll in mud to keep cool.

Pigs form close bonds with other pigs. Bonded pigs often sleep nose to nose.

ARE YOU A GENIUS KID?

You now know plenty of facts about pigs. Your friends and family are sure to be wowed! But are you ready to share your knowledge? First, let's test what you have learned.

Check back through the book if you are not sure.

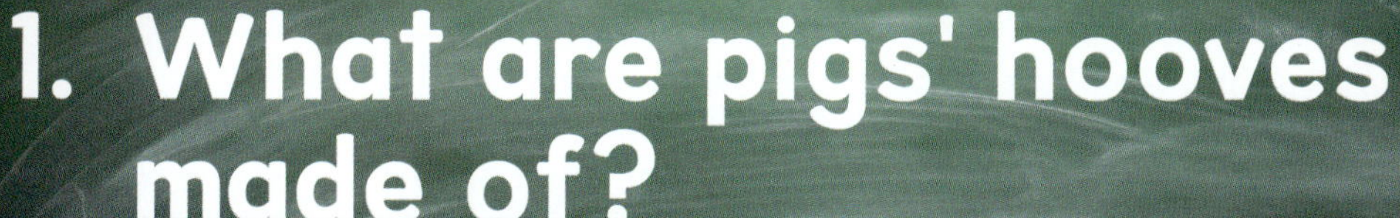

1. What are pigs' hooves made of?
2. Where do most farm pigs live?
3. Why do pigs roll in mud?

Answers:
1. keratin
2. in barns
3. to keep cool

GLOSSARY

bonds relationships based on love, friendship, and loyalty

breeds groups of animals that are bred to have similar characteristics

characteristics features of a living thing that help to identify it

communicate to share information

habitats the natural homes in which plants, animals, and other living things live

vaccinate to inject medicine into a person or animal to protect against a disease

INDEX